Get ready to go diving! In this book se[e] most monstrous creatures of the dee[p] life with a few clicks of the mouse…

Monsters of the Deep uses augmented reality (AR) technology to set free some truly awesome animals and send them swimming right up to your screen. **Here's what to do:**

1  Check that your computer has a **webcam** and that it can run the downloadable augmented reality (AR) software (see the **Minimum System Requirements** panel opposite).

2  Go to *http://kids.nationalgeographic.com/monstersofthedeep* to download the **software.** Choose Mac or PC as appropriate for your computer, then double-click on the downloaded software file to start the program.

3  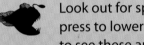 As you go through the book, look out for this symbol which shows you're on a **special AR page.** Once you see that the software is running, hold each 3-D action card in front of your webcam. Now watch the amazing ocean creatures come to life!

TOP DEEP-SEA DIVING TIPS

 Look out for special keys you can press to lower you into the ocean to see these animals up close.

 Press other special keys on your keyboard for access to amazing video clips and fact-file slide shows.

 To view full screen, click the green button on the AR window. To close the window, click the red cross.

 For the best underwater animation experience, avoid having too much light reflecting off the action cards.

Make sure your computer speakers are turned up high!

Need some help?

If you've got a problem, check out our website for troubleshooting information:

http://kids.nationalgeographic.com/monstersofthedeep

The publishers would like to thank the following sources for their kind permission to reproduce the pictures in this book.

PICTURE CREDITS

Key: t: top, b: bottom, l: left, r: right.

Alamy: /Peter Arnold: 30tr, /Sabena Jane Blackbird: 11tr, /Simon Margetson Travel: 10/11c

Corbis: /Bettmann: 30bl, /Clouds Hill Imaging: 6bl, /Denis Scott: 6/7c, 14/15c, 26/27c / Mike Theiss/Ultimate Chase: 8br

FLPA: /Flip Nicklin/Minden Pictures: 7r, Norbert Wu/Minden Pictures: 28, 29bl, 29br

Getty Images: 25bl, /Gary Bell: CD label,16/17c, /Jeff Foott/Discover Channel Images: 8b, /Tim Graham: 16c, /Justin Lewis/Image Bank: 23br, /Emory Kristof/National Geographic: 31r, /David Liittschwager/National Geographic: 13r, /Popperfoto: 26tr

Nature Picture Library: De Meester/Arco: 27b, /Mark Carwardine: 15t, /David Fleetham: 23r, /Jurgen Freund: 17br, 19br, /Steven Kazlowski: 14b, /Todd Pusser: 9r, /Andy Rouse: 18/19c, /Tom Walmsley: 12b, /Doc White: 14br, 22l, 29bc, /Rod Williams: 20br

NHPA: 20bl, /A.N.T. Photo Library: 18br, /Franco Banfi: 13b, /Image Quest 3D: 18bl, / James Carmichael Junior: 11bl, /Oceans Image: 12/13c, /Oceans Image/Photoshot: 3tl, 8l, 8/9c, 16bl, 17tr, 22br, 22/23c, 26bl

Photolibrary.com: /Reinhard Dirscherl: 4/5c, /Jeffrey L. Rottman: 11br

Seapics.com: /Kat Bolstad: 24bl, 29br

AR ACTIVATION CARDS

Great White Shark: Denis Scott/Corbis
Blue Whale: Denis Scott/Corbis
Manta Ray: Oceans Image/Photoshot/NHPA
Blackdevil Angler Fish: Norbert Wu/Minden Pictures/FLPA

AR Shark (video footage: Image Bank Film/Getty Images)
Whale Shark: Doug Perrine/Nature Picture Library
Tiger Shark: Mike Parry/Minden Pictures/FLPA
Hammerhead Shark: Fred Bavendam/Minden Pictures/FLPA
Grey Reef Shark: Reinhard Dirscherl/FLPA
Bull Shark: Flip Nicklin/Minden Pictures/FLP
Basking Shark: Alan James/Nature Picture Library

AR Whale (video footage: BBC Motion Gallery)
Minke & Grey Whale: Mark Carwardine/Nature Picture Library
Bowhead Whale: Martha Holmes/Nature Picture Library
Fin Whale: Doc White/Nature Picture Library
Humpback Whale: Brandon Cole/Nature Picture Library
Sei Whale: Doug Perrine/Nature Picture Library

AR Ray (video footage: Corbis)
Giant Devil Ray: Reinhard Dirscherl/NHPA
Large Tooth Saw Fish: Paulo de Oliveira/Photolibrary.com
Common Torpedo Fish: Burt Jones & Maurine Shimlock/NHPA
Spotted Eagle Ray: Peter Oxford/Nature Picture Library
Southern Stingray: Tom & Therisa Stack/NHPA

AR Angler Fish (video footage: BBC Motion Gallery)
Ogre Fish: David Shale/Nature Picture Library
Whiptail Gulper: Norbert Wu/Minden Pictures/Getty Images
Vampire Squid: Steve Downer/Ardea
Narrownose Chimera: David Shale/Nature Picture Library
Viperfish: David Shale/Nature Picture Library
Triplewart Seadevil: Norbert Wu/Minden Pictures/FLPA

CD folder: iStock

Published by the National Geographic Society, Washington, D.C. 20036. Design copyright © Carlton Books Limited 2011. Text copyright © Nicola Davies 2011. All rights reserved. Reproduction in whole or in part without written permission of the publisher is strictly prohibited.

The right of Carlton Books Limited to be identified as Proprietor of this work has been asserted in accordance with the Copyright, Design and Patents Act 1988.

ISBN: 978-1-4263-0860-4
Printed in Heshan, China   11/CAR/1

Carlton Books
Executive Editor: Barry Timms
Senior Art Editor: Jake DaCosta
Designer: Ceri Woods
Photoshop Illustrator: Ryan Forshaw
Creative Director: Clare Baggaley
Picture Research: Ben White
Production: Claire Hayward

National Geographic Society
Project Editor: Rebecca Baines
Design Director: Jonathan Halling
Art Director: Eva Absher
Production Assistant: Kathryn Robbins
Associate Managing Editor: Grace Hill
Editorial Assistant: Kate Olesin

MONSTERS
OF THE DEEP

Nicola Davies

Dear Reader:

The dictionary defines a monster as a creature that is "typically" large, ugly, or frightening and also "imaginary." But in our oceans there are real creatures that are more monstrous than anything you could ever imagine. This book is going to take you so close to them, you'll feel that they are in the room with you.

I'm sure you won't be scared, because I expect you already know that real creatures have very good reasons for being big, ugly, or scary—reasons that are key to surviving in their ocean environment. Once you know these facts, these animals will stop being monsters and start to become amazing beasts that you'll want to know more about. Read on to begin your deep-sea discoveries.

Nicola Davies

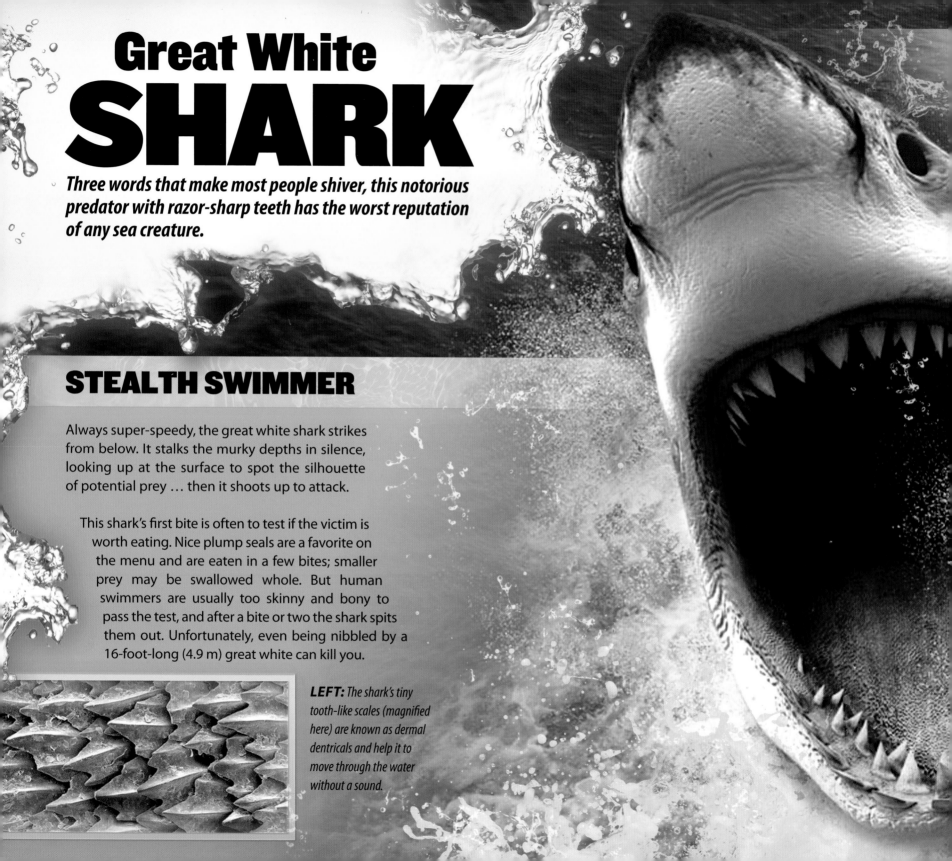

Great White
SHARK

Three words that make most people shiver, this notorious predator with razor-sharp teeth has the worst reputation of any sea creature.

STEALTH SWIMMER

Always super-speedy, the great white shark strikes from below. It stalks the murky depths in silence, looking up at the surface to spot the silhouette of potential prey ... then it shoots up to attack.

This shark's first bite is often to test if the victim is worth eating. Nice plump seals are a favorite on the menu and are eaten in a few bites; smaller prey may be swallowed whole. But human swimmers are usually too skinny and bony to pass the test, and after a bite or two the shark spits them out. Unfortunately, even being nibbled by a 16-foot-long (4.9 m) great white can kill you.

LEFT: The shark's tiny tooth-like scales (magnified here) are known as dermal dentricals and help it to move through the water without a sound.

BIG, BRUTAL BITES

A shark is never without its bite. Its teeth are arranged in rows, one behind the other, so that if a tooth is lost it is replaced immediately by another. Sharks go through thousands of them in a lifetime, which is why so many teeth have been found.

A great white's teeth are razor sharp; their triangular shape makes them strong. Baby teeth are replaced by adult teeth as the shark ages. Young great whites have narrow teeth—good for grabbing small, slippery prey and swallowing them whole. Adults have shorter, wider teeth—with enough strength to slice through the flesh and bone of seals and other big mammals.

RIGHT: The tooth of the great white shark has sharp, serrated edges, like a steak knife.

① LET'S GO DIVING!

- TO PREPARE FOR YOUR DIVE, HOLD THE SHARK 3-D ACTION CARD UP TO YOUR WEBCAM.
- TO LOWER THE DIVING CAGE, PRESS THE **RETURN** KEY ON YOUR KEYBOARD.
- TO SEARCH FOR SHARKS, **ROTATE** THE ACTION CARD TO THE LEFT AND RIGHT.
- PRESS THE **LEFT** KEY ON YOUR KEYBOARD TO WATCH A VIDEO OF THE GREAT WHITE SHARK.
- PRESS THE **RIGHT** KEY, THEN THE **NUMBER** KEYS, TO DISCOVER OTHER TYPES OF SHARKS.

KILLER SENSES

Three main senses help the great white to track down its prey...

Smell

A shark's nose is so sensitive it could detect a drop of blood in a swimming pool. The difference in smell strength between its left and right nostrils helps it to tell where a scent comes from. A series of tiny pores along the shark's body, called the lateral line, detects the slightest ripple in the water. This information might tell the shark where a scent-bearing current is coming from, or if prey is moving nearby.

Sight

Just like humans, a shark's pupils change size in bright or dim light to help filter the light. But in low light their sight is ten times better than ours. Movements that might look blurred to humans are sharp to the great white's eye, which would notice each of the 25 individual pictures that make up one second of a film.

Electrical sense

All living creatures have nerves, which work by sending electrical messages. Sharks use this electricity to find prey hidden in the darkness. Gel-filled pits on the great white's snout can sense the tiny electrical charges of nearby living creatures, and even the magnetic fields of rocks on which seals and other prey might be resting.

SIZE

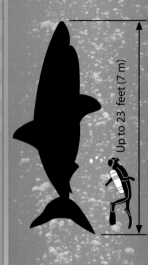

Up to 23 feet (7 m)

DEPTH FT(M)

0 (0)

300 (91)

650 (198)

1,000 (305)

1,300 (396)

1,650 (503)

Often near the surface but regularly dive down to 1,000 feet (305 m)

LOCATION

Almost anywhere that the sea is warmer than 50°F (10°C)

ORCA

Like black-and-white torpedoes, orcas slice through the waves. Also known as killer whales, they are the wolves of the sea, taking on any prey they choose—even whales twice their size.

ABOVE: *Dorsal fins can be seven feet (2 m) high on the biggest male orcas.*

TOP SPEED

An orca is easy to spot at sea, with its striking black-and-white pattern and a black dorsal fin rising up from its back. It cruises for hours at around six miles an hour (9.6 kph). In short bursts of speed it can reach up to 30 miles an hour (48 kph)! Not bad for an animal that can grow to 32 feet long (9.8 m) and weigh over five tons.

We are family

Orca babies, or calves, usually stay with their pod for their whole lives, which can be 50 to 100 years. They learn the special hunting techniques of their pod from the adults around them. Different pods sometimes get together—perhaps teaming up for a special hunt, or mingling just to socialize. This gives orcas the chance to find a mate outside of their own family.

Captive killers

You may have seen orcas in captivity performing spectacular tricks, but many have been taken from their families in the wild. They might seem fine and may even breed, but for animals used to roaming the open sea, even the biggest tank is confining.

TEAMWORK

Size, strength, and speed help to make orcas one of the sea's top predators, but the other key to their success is teamwork. They live in family groups called pods and work together to hunt their prey. Each pod knows exactly where and when to catch its chosen victims and the best way to cooperate to make the hunt a success.

Some pods hunt by herding schools of fish, while others ride waves onto beaches to grab seal pups. There are also those that chase whales over huge distances until they are too tired to protect themselves.

ABOVE: *Orcas live and hunt together in family groups called pods.*

 ## Team talk

Teamwork relies on good communication, and orcas make lots of different sounds— whistles, squeaks, and screeches—to talk to each other. Each pod has its own special vocabulary of noises, allowing scientists to tell one pod from another.

Orcas also make clicking sounds that help them to find their way through water too dark to see in. They listen to the echoes of these clicks and get a picture in sound of everything around them. This is called echolocation, and almost all whales and dolphins use it to navigate in their underwater world. If you get close to these creatures in a canoe or small boat you can sometimes hear their clicks through the hull.

SIZE

Up to 32 feet (9.8 m)

DEPTH FT(M)

0(0)

300(91)

650(198)

1,000(305)

1,300(396)

1,650(503)

Can dive down to lower depths

LOCATION

All the oceans of the world

Giant Japanese
SPIDER CRAB

Meet a crab with fearsome pincers and legs so long it could cuddle a small car! No wonder there are stories of it feasting on the bodies of drowned sailors.

BIG... BIGGER...

The biggest giant Japanese spider crab on record measured 12 feet (3.7 m) from tip to tip of its longest, pincer-carrying forelegs. At over 40 pounds (18 kg), it weighed about the same as a medium-size dog! But as with all sea monsters, there are stories of even bigger spider crabs.

In 1921, fishermen on Honshu Island, in Japan, claimed they caught a crab with a 19-foot (5.8 m) leg span. And back in 1886, European visitors to a Japanese fishing village said that they saw 10-foot-long (3 m) spider crab legs propped up outside a fisherman's hut. If their story was true, those legs belonged to a crab with a leg span of 22 feet (6.7 m)—big enough to wrap around a pickup truck!

BIGGEST?

Could there be bigger crabs lurking in the depths with 60-foot (18 m) leg spans and bodies that weigh over 200 pounds (91 kg)? The answer is probably "no" because of the way spider crab bodies are put together.

Crabs belong to a group of animals called arthropods, which also includes spiders. Arthropods have jointed legs, like drinking straws joined together with elastic bands. These work well for small creatures but not for big ones. A 200-pound (91 kg) spider crab simply wouldn't be able to walk with such spindly legs and weak joints. But even at 12 feet (3.7 m), Japanese spider crabs are still the biggest arthropods on Earth. Watch out for them if you ever go for a dive off the coast of Japan!

Sand sifters

Despite their impressive size, giant Japanese spider crabs are rather gentle creatures. They putter around the seafloor, sifting through the sand with their pincers to find worms, sponges, and other small creatures, which they then pass to their mouths—just like if you were trying to feed yourself with barbeque tongs!

Like many species of crab, spider crabs are also scavengers—meaning they eat anything dead they find. They perform a useful garbage disposal service by eating dead plants and animal bodies that sink to the seafloor.

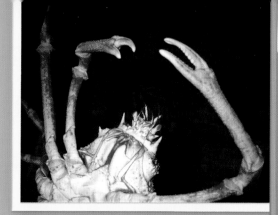

ABOVE: Japanese spider crabs use their pincers to pass food to their mouths.

Aliens!

Of course, Japanese spider crabs aren't born giants! They start life as tiny larvae, small as a pinprick, floating with the plankton at the surface of the sea. They don't even look like crabs at this stage—more like tiny space aliens.

Gradually the spider crab babies change into their adult shape and sink to the seafloor, but it takes them many years to grow into giants. They may live to be 100 years old, making them not just one of the biggest, but also one of the longest living creatures of the deep.

ABOVE: When compared directly with a human adult, you can see just what a giant the Japanese spider crab is!

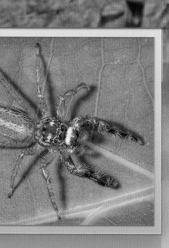

ABOVE: Like spiders and insects, crabs belong to a group of animals called arthropods.

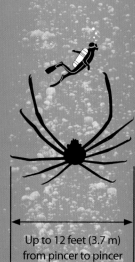

SIZE

Up to 12 feet (3.7 m) from pincer to pincer

DEPTH FT(M)

0(0)

650(198)

1,300(396)

2,000(610)

2,600(792)

3,300(1006)

Can be found as deep as 2,600 feet (792 m)

LOCATION

Pacific waters, off the coast of Japan

Ocean
SUNFISH

With a big round body and a strange frill where a normal fish tail should be, the ocean sunfish is not only giant—it's weird too!

BIG AND BONY

A normal-size adult sunfish, or "mola," is huge. Weighing over a ton, it's almost six feet (1.8 m) in length and about eight feet (2.4 m) from fin to fin. But the biggest sunfish can be much larger.

In 1908 the *S.S. Fiona*'s propeller struck an enormous sunfish outside Sydney harbor, Australia. It was over ten feet (3 m) long and weighed almost three tons! This makes the ocean sunfish the heaviest bony fish in the sea (unlike sharks and rays whose skeletons are made of cartilage).

ABOVE: *A sunfish bathes in the sun's rays to warm up its body after a dive into the cold depths.*

SLOW AND STEADY

Ocean sunfish are great travelers, crossing thousands of miles of ocean in their lifetime. It's hard to imagine how such a big round body can swim so far with just two little fins. Sunfish are slow, but keep a steady pace and can cover 16 miles (26 km) in a day.

Whenever sunfish dive down through cold waters in search of food, they need to warm up afterward. They do this by sunbathing at the surface—a behavior that has earned them their common name.

On the menu

Ocean sunfish mostly eat jellyfish, which they suck in and out of their mouths, much like a person would blow a bubblegum bubble. This process, plus two pairs of beak-like teeth in its mouth and some extra teeth in its throat, helps to break the jellyfish into bits. It also makes ocean sunfish very vulnerable to choking on discarded plastic bags, which look just like juicy jellyfish when in the water.

THE CLEANING STATION

Ocean sunfish are used to wandering the oceans alone, but they do meet others of their kind at "cleaning stations." Sunfish carry lots of parasites—more than 40 different kinds—so they sometimes stop for small "cleaner fish" to gobble up the parasites off their bodies. Sometimes there can be as many as a dozen sunfish waiting for a turn!

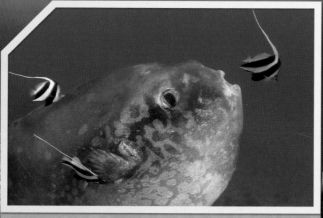

ABOVE: *A sunfish keeps clean and parasite free by allowing other fish to feast on the small creatures it carries.*

Oh baby!

Adult sunfish have thick rubbery skin that protects their big round bodies. But many baby sunfish wind up as dinner before they reach adulthood. This could be why females can lay 300 million eggs at a time!

Baby sunfish look like nine-pointed stars and grow really fast, increasing their weight a whopping 60 million times before reaching adulthood. That's like a tadpole growing into a frog the size of a truck!

ABOVE: *A baby sunfish is star shaped and very vulnerable to predators that might eat it, despite the many spines covering its body.*

SIZE

Up to 10.5 feet (3.2 m)

DEPTH FT (M)

0 (0)

300 (91)

650 (198)

1,000 (305)

1,300 (396)

1,650 (503)

Usually near the surface but can dive down to 650 feet (198 m)

LOCATION

All tropical and temperate oceans in waters warmer than 50°F (10°C)

Blue
WHALE

A blue whale is as long as three buses and weighs the same as 83 great white sharks! Everything about this massive mammal is truly monstrous.

Noisy neighbors

Blue whales are usually alone when you see them in the ocean, but this doesn't mean that they're lonely. They keep in touch with each other by making a variety of deep moaning and humming sounds. Some sounds are too low for human ears to detect and some are louder than a jet aircraft taking off. These sounds are known to travel through hundreds of miles of open ocean.

BIG-HEARTED

When you see a blue whale in the ocean, its long back seems to go on forever! At around 100 feet (30 m) long, it's the biggest animal ever to have lived on Earth. Nearly twice as heavy as the largest dinosaur known to man, this creature has a heart the size of a small car.

This huge heart pumps over 11 tons of blood through 62,000 miles (99,780 k) of blood vessels, some of them big enough for a person to swim through. It's so large, it beats only five or six times a minute.

RIGHT: *The pleated throat of the blue whale expands to take in a whole school of krill in one big gulp.*

LEFT: *Blue whales can eat up to million krill a day.*

Mega baby

A newborn blue whale, or calf, is 24 feet (7.3 m) in length—longer than an SUV! But it doesn't stay this size for long. Drinking 132 gallons (500 l) of Mom's milk a day makes the blue whale calf grow about eight pounds (3.6 kg) every hour! By the time the calf is six months old, it is over 19 tons heavier than when it was born, and nearly twice as long.

TINY FOOD

Blue whales may be enormous but their food is not. They feed on krill—shrimp-like creatures about the size of your pinky. It takes a lot of krill to feed a blue whale, and luckily they swarm together in schools, or groups, of millions of krill. Pleats in the blue whale's throat open out when it feeds, allowing it to swallow a whole school in one gulp.

The whale then sieves the krill from the water using its baleen plates. Each plate is like a giant, bristly dagger, and hundreds of them grow, one behind the other, from the whale's upper jaw. Their overlapping bristles allow the gulped water to flow back out while trapping the krill inside the whale's mouth.

2 LET'S GO DIVING!

- TO PREPARE FOR YOUR DIVE, HOLD THE BLUE WHALE 3-D ACTION CARD UP TO YOUR WEBCAM.
- TO DIVE DOWN INTO THE OCEAN, PRESS THE *RETURN* KEY ON YOUR KEYBOARD.
- TO SEARCH FOR THE BLUE WHALE, *ROTATE* THE ACTION CARD TO THE LEFT AND RIGHT.
- PRESS THE *LEFT* KEY ON YOUR KEYBOARD TO WATCH A VIDEO OF THE BLUE WHALE.
- PRESS THE *RIGHT* KEY, THEN THE *NUMBER* KEYS, TO DISCOVER OTHER TYPES OF WHALES.

SIZE

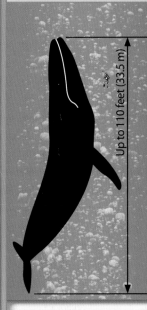

Up to 110 feet (33.5 m)

DEPTH FT(M)

0 (0)

300 (91)

650 (198)

1,000 (305)

1,300 (396)

1,650 (503)

About 200 feet (61 m) but can dive as deep as 1,650 feet (503 m)

LOCATION

All the oceans of the world

Box
JELLYFISH

The toxic killers of the Australian Barrier Reef, box jellyfish can be as big as a hat or smaller than a fingertip, but all have stings that can kill a human in minutes…

DEADLY TO HUMANS

Humans aren't on the box jellyfish menu but the touch of a single tentacle can be enough to kill a person. The cocktail of poisons in a box jelly sting causes muscle cramps, damages nerves, and eats through skin, leading to terrible pain, paralysis, and heart failure in humans.

Some victims die of shock or drowning before they even reach the shore. This has led scientists to believe that many deaths previously thought to have been caused by drowning or heart attacks were in fact the result of deadly box jelly encounters.

LEFT: A seaside sign warns bathers of the risk of box jellyfish stings. Don't swim where you see this sign!

SUPERFAST KILLERS

Box jellies aren't really jellyfish at all. They are relatives of the animals we usually call by that name. Real jellyfish are slow-moving creatures that drift with the waves, but box jellyfish are fast-swimming, active predators.

Though fragile as paper, box jellyfish are the deadliest creatures in the sea, each with up to 60 stinging tentacles and a big appetite. They eat fish, and, to avoid having their delicate bodies ripped apart by the struggles of their prey, box jellyfish must kill their meal before their meal kills them. Each tentacle can carry 30,000 stinging cells, which fire like arrows and inject enough lethal poison to kill fish instantly.

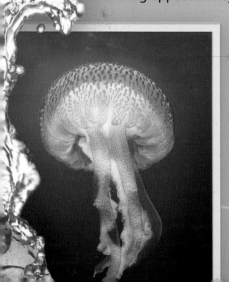

LEFT: A real jellyfish like this one moves slowly and is only a relative of the fast-swimming box jellyfish.

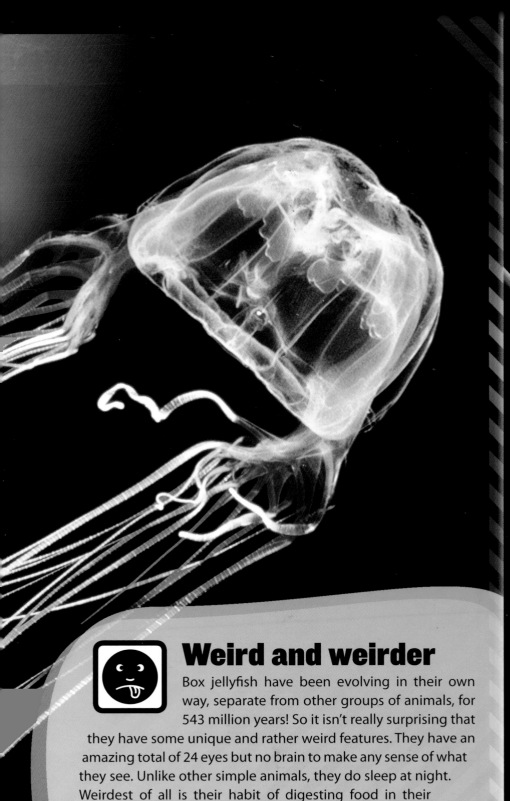

Survivors' secrets

There's one animal on which box jellyfish have no effect at all. Sea turtles eat box jellies as part of their diet but aren't harmed by their stings. The reason is a mystery, but solving it in the future could help scientists come up with an antivenom.

Coming soon to a sea near you...

There are 36 different kinds of box jellyfish, with scientists discovering new species every year. The biggest and most deadly is the hat-size "sea wasp," which has ten-foot-long (3 m) tentacles. But smaller peanut-size species can cause Irukandji syndrome —intense pain and raised blood pressure that can put victims in the hospital or even cause death.

Box jellies appear to be spreading. No longer found only in the tropical waters of the Pacific and Indian Oceans, they are now showing up in parts of the Atlantic and Mediterranean too. There's no antidote to box jellyfish stings yet, but vinegar can stop any untriggered stinging cells from firing.

ABOVE: *A peanut-size box jellyfish attacks a tiny fish.*

Weird and weirder

Box jellyfish have been evolving in their own way, separate from other groups of animals, for 543 million years! So it isn't really surprising that they have some unique and rather weird features. They have an amazing total of 24 eyes but no brain to make any sense of what they see. Unlike other simple animals, they do sleep at night. Weirdest of all is their habit of digesting food in their tentacles and then excreting it out the ends!

SIZE

Up to 10.5 feet (3.2 m)

DEPTH FT(M)

0(0)

300(91)

650(198)

1,000(305)

1,300(396)

1,650(503)

Found in shallow coastal waters

LOCATION

Mainly the Pacific and Indian Oceans, but spreading

Whale
SHARK

Imagine a shark as long as a bus swimming toward you, with a mouth wide enough to swallow a sofa. It's a whale shark— but you're way too big to be its dinner!

SUPER SIEVER

Giant sharks need a giant amount of food. Luckily, whale sharks, like many of the sea's largest creatures, eat huge portions of a food that's small but very plentiful: plankton.

Plankton is like a soup of plants and animals, and to get nourishment from this soup, whale sharks have a filter system. Sieves made of skin line their throats and gills, and when a whale shark sucks in water, these sieves hold on to anything bigger than a pinhead. Whale sharks can eat small fish, too, if they are nicely bunched together and easy to gulp!

BELOW: Plankton are microscopic plants and animals that live in the oceans of the world.

Shark soup?

All over the world, many types of shark are under threat from humans who kill them and use them to make soup, polish, food, leather, lipsticks, pet food, and even souvenirs. Whale sharks are targeted by some commercial fishing operations. Despite their endangered status, hunting these gentle giants is still legal in parts of the world.

MYSTERIOUS WANDERERS

Whale sharks must wander to find their food, sometimes traveling thousands of miles in a year. Where plankton is plentiful, many whale sharks will gather to feed, but when the plankton bloom is over, the whale sharks disappear. Despite their size, these giant creatures are very mysterious animals that we don't know much about. For instance, although we know they give birth to live babies, we can only guess where in the world it happens!

Spots and stripes

Scientists are trying hard to answer some of the questions about how whale sharks live and where they go. Fortunately the pattern of spots and stripes on a whale shark's body is unique and identifies each one as clearly as your face identifies you.

By taking photos of their skin patterns in different parts of the world, scientists from the ECOCEAN whale shark identification project track each shark to see where it turns up. They compare every new photo with thousands of photos already on their records. This would take a long time by hand, but ECOCEAN uses computer software invented by astronomers to map the stars to help them find photos in which the whale shark spot patterns match. Divers and ecotourists add to the research by sending in their whale shark pictures.

ABOVE: *Each whale shark's pattern of spots and stripes is as unique as your own face.*

SIZE

Up to 40 feet (12.2 m)

DEPTH FT(M)

0(0)

300(91)

650(198)

1,000(305)

1,300(396)

1,650(503)

Often near the surface but can dive down to 2,300 feet (701 m)

LOCATION

All tropical and warm temperate waters

Giant Tube
WORMS

In the depths of the pitch black water where vents in the ocean floor spew boiling water out of the Earth's crust, the giant tube worm is right at home.

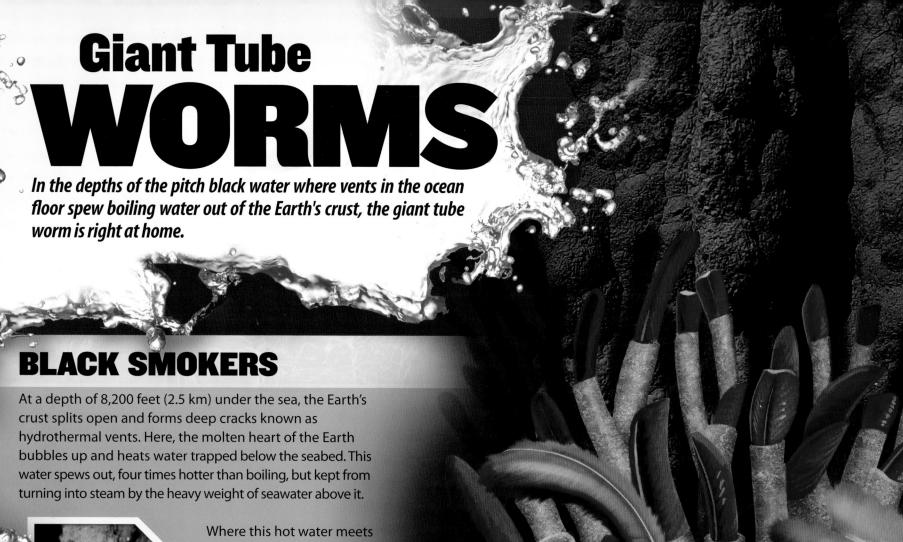

BLACK SMOKERS

At a depth of 8,200 feet (2.5 km) under the sea, the Earth's crust splits open and forms deep cracks known as hydrothermal vents. Here, the molten heart of the Earth bubbles up and heats water trapped below the seabed. This water spews out, four times hotter than boiling, but kept from turning into steam by the heavy weight of seawater above it.

Where this hot water meets the cold water of the deep ocean, towers of black toxic chemicals form, with dark water spouting from their chimney-like tops. These are called black smokers, and around them, where the water isn't quite so hot, are colonies of tube worms, like fields of underwater flowers. How can anything live in such a inhospitable place?

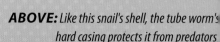

ABOVE: *Like this snail's shell, the tube worm's hard casing protects it from predators*

MILLIONS OF HELPERS

Each giant tube worm has a long white body with a red plume at its end. It has no eyes, no mouth, and no stomach. The red pigment in its plume is the same as the one in your blood that carries oxygen around your body. But for the giant tube worm it soaks up chemicals from the hydrothermal vent to feed to billions of bacteria that live inside the worm.

In return for being fed and housed, the bacteria make food for the worm. This kind of relationship where two types of animals both benefit from working together is called symbiosis. It works so well that tube worms can grow to be seven feet (2.1 m) long in just 18 months.

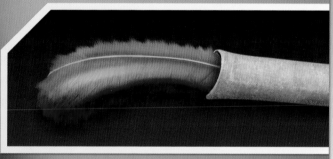

ABOVE: *The red plume at the end of each worm soaks up valuable chemicals from the hydrothermal vent.*

Protective armor

tube worm's tough tube is made of the same stuff s an insect's exoskeleton. When tube worms feel a ovement in the water they wiggle inside, like a ail pulling itself inside its shell for protection. ut the worms aren't always quick enough to cape the armies of shrimp, crab, and fish that ant to eat them. Far away from our world of nlight, tube worms are the start of an undersea od chain.

Endings and beginnings

Hydrothermal vents don't last forever. If the split in the Earth's crust closes over, all the tube worms and the life they support will die. But somewhere else on the ocean floor another split will open up, and tiny tube worm larvae will take up residence. Unlike the grown-up worms, these larvae have mouths so they can swallow their friendly bacteria. Then they start to grow, without eating or seeing at all, down in the dark depths.

SIZE

Up to 7 feet (2.1 m)

DEPTH FT(M)

0(0)

1,600(488)

3,200(975)

5,000(1524)

6,600(2012)

8,200(2500)

8,200 feet (2.5 km) deep and below

LOCATION

Only in the deepest oceans around hydrothermal vents.

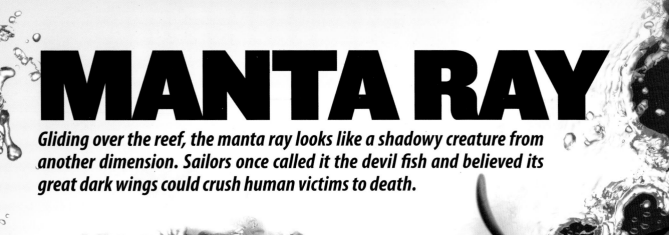

MANTA RAY

Gliding over the reef, the manta ray looks like a shadowy creature from another dimension. Sailors once called it the devil fish and believed its great dark wings could crush human victims to death.

ABOVE: *In spite of their size, manta rays are agile swimmers. They can even jump right out of the ocean, which is known as breaching.*

FIN WINGS

In reality, manta rays are gentle giants, harmless plankton feeders and one of the most graceful creatures of the deep. They are related to sharks, and their huge wings—which can measure 25 feet (7.6 m) from tip to tip—are actually big, flat pectoral fins. Mantas swim by slowly flapping and can travel hundreds of miles in just a few days to find food, a mate, or a safe place to breed.

3 LET'S GO DIVING!

- TO PREPARE FOR YOUR DIVE, HOLD THE MANTA RAY 3-D ACTION CARD UP TO YOUR WEBCAM.
- TO DIVE DOWN INTO THE OCEAN, PRESS THE **RETURN** KEY ON YOUR KEYBOARD.
- TO SEARCH FOR MANTA RAYS, **ROTATE** THE ACTION CARD TO THE LEFT AND RIGHT.
- PRESS THE **LEFT** KEY ON YOUR KEYBOARD TO WATCH A VIDEO OF THE MANTA RAY.
- PRESS THE **RIGHT** KEY, THEN THE **NUMBER** KEYS, TO DISCOVER CREATURES RELATED TO THE MANTA.

Mantas in danger

Sharks and killer whales like to make a meal of manta rays, and even the largest adults carry scars from close encounters. One reason mantas can survive these attacks is that their wounds are attended to by "cleaner fish," who specialize in eating the dead or infected skin—as well as the parasites—of other animals. However, thousands of manta rays are killed by humans every year for their gills, which are used in medicines, and their fins, which are used more and more in shark-fin soup as sharks become more endangered.

EATING AND BREATHING

Two horn-like fins on the manta's head funnel water into its mouth, over its gills and out again through the gill slits on its underside. Like all fish, mantas breathe water through their gills. But manta gills do another job, too: they are covered with a sticky, spongy layer that captures tiny sea creatures and fish eggs for the manta to eat. Manta ray food doesn't need chewing, so this creature's 300 teeth are just tiny specks without a real job!

ABOVE: *The gill slits of the manta ray filter both oxygen and food from the seawater.*

The tell tail

Manta rays are related to stingrays. One way to tell different species of rays apart is by the size and shape of their "stinger"—the poisonous spine at the end of their tails. Studying manta ray stings has shown that there are actually two different species of manta. The biggest mantas wander over thousands of miles of ocean and still have the remains of a stinger—just like their stingray relatives. But the smaller, more homebody kind of mantas don't have any stinger at all.

ABOVE: *The stingray is a relative of the much larger manta ray.*

SIZE

Up to 25 feet (7.6 m)

DEPTH FT(M)

0(0)

300(91)

650(198)

1,000(305)

1,300(396)

1,650(503)

Often near the surface but sometimes dive deeper.

LOCATION

Tropical oceans, often near coral reefs

Colossal
SQUID

Large enough to go head to head with 40-ton sperm whales, the colossal squid was thought to be just a seafarer's story for most of the 20th century.

REAL OR IMAGINARY?

Just like its slightly smaller cousin, the giant squid, the colossal squid was believed to be an imaginary creature for many years. The first signs of this monster appeared in 1925, when whalers found two vast tentacles in the stomach of a sperm whale. They were bigger, thicker, and more deadly than the tentacles of the more familiar giant squid, which at that time was thought to be the biggest squid in the ocean. What could these huge tentacles possibly belong to?

Not until this century have live specimens been found and photographed. In 2003, a colossal squid was caught alive by fishermen in the Antarctic Ocean and brought to New Zealand for scientific analysis. The body of this creature was around 8 feet (2.4 m) long—a monstrous fact in itself. But the scientists concluded that it was a youngster, only two-thirds grown. Had it lived to become an adult, its body would have been 13 feet (4 m) in length!

LEFT: *A scientist examines the sharp hooks on the colossal squid's tentacles, which can swivel to dig into the flesh of its victims.*

DEEP-SEA WARS

The colossal squid is a deep pinky-red color. In the depths where it lives, light cannot penetrate, so it remains almost invisible to unsuspecting victims. The colossal squid has two extra-long prey-catching tentacles that are covered with needle-sharp hooks. It is big and powerful enough to go after really huge fish, such as the seven-foot-long (2.1 m), 450-pound (204 kg) Patagonian tooth fish.

So how might this giant react to an attack from a sperm whale? We can only guess. But the evidence suggests that it would put up a good fight because some sperm whales carry the scars of those swiveling hooks. The squid probably wouldn't win, however. Squid beaks have been found in large male sperm whale stomachs, and from the size of these hooks we know that there must be squid more colossal than any human has ever seen! With bodies 16 feet (4.9 m) long and 65 feet (20 m) of tentacles, these ten-armed monsters are down there somewhere, ending up as sperm whale dinners.

Deep-sea discoveries

In 2007, the crew of a boat fishing in Antarctic waters pulled up a colossal squid on their fishing line. This monster wouldn't let go of the fish they'd caught, and was scooped up in a net. The fishermen stored the squid in the boat's freezer and took it back to New Zealand for biologists to measure.

ABOVE: *A colossal squid is pulled aboard a fishing boat in Antarctic waters.*

ABOVE: *Like all other types of squid, the colossal squid has horny jaws that look just like a parrot's beak.*

SIZE

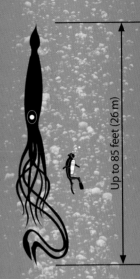

Up to 85 feet (26 m)

DEPTH FT(M)

0 (0)

650 (198)

1,300 (396)

2,000 (610)

2,600 (792)

3,300 (1006)

3,300 feet (1 km) deep and below

LOCATION

Antarctic Ocean

Sperm
WHALE

A huge triangle-shaped tail disappears beneath the ocean's surface. It's a sperm whale, diving down into the mysterious depths. Listen and you'll hear its clicking sounds.

ABOVE: *Long ago seafarers told tales of these ma mammals that would destroy their boats.*

BIG TALKERS

A diving sperm whale sounds rather like a ticking clock. It clicks and listens to the echos to find its way around, just like the orca whale does. Sperm whales are very sociable creatures and also use their clicks for communication with others of their species.

Clicks are so important to the sperm whale that almost all of its huge barrel-shaped head is devoted to making them. The head takes up a third of its body length and is packed full of an oily substance called spermaceti, plus air sacs and tubes. Together these allow the whale to make powerful, complicated sounds.

DEEP-SEA DIVERS

Sperm whales are air-breathing mammals like us, but can dive to depths of up to 9,000 feet (2.7 km) below the surface. They stay down there for up to 90 minutes at a time!

Deep breaths at the surface before a dive let the sperm whale store enough oxygen in its blood and muscles to hold its breath while it dives—a bit like charging a battery. But when the whale comes up from a long dive, it must rest before diving again.

ABOVE: *Sperm whales have the largest brain of any animal on Earth.*

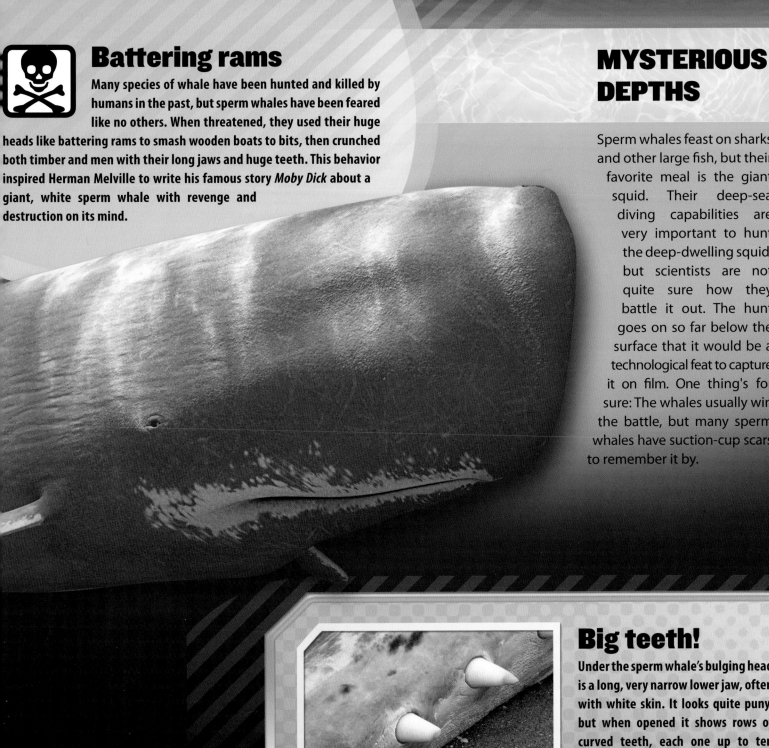

Battering rams

Many species of whale have been hunted and killed by humans in the past, but sperm whales have been feared like no others. When threatened, they used their huge heads like battering rams to smash wooden boats to bits, then crunched both timber and men with their long jaws and huge teeth. This behavior inspired Herman Melville to write his famous story *Moby Dick* about a giant, white sperm whale with revenge and destruction on its mind.

MYSTERIOUS DEPTHS

Sperm whales feast on sharks and other large fish, but their favorite meal is the giant squid. Their deep-sea diving capabilities are very important to hunt the deep-dwelling squid, but scientists are not quite sure how they battle it out. The hunt goes on so far below the surface that it would be a technological feat to capture it on film. One thing's for sure: The whales usually win the battle, but many sperm whales have suction-cup scars to remember it by.

Big teeth!

Under the sperm whale's bulging head is a long, very narrow lower jaw, often with white skin. It looks quite puny, but when opened it shows rows of curved teeth, each one up to ten inches (25 cm) long and weighing up to one pound (.5 kg)—perfect for grabbing the biggest and most slippery prey.

SIZE

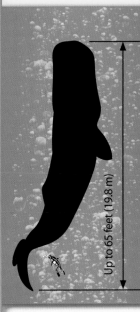

Up to 65 feet (19.8 m)

DEPTH FT(M)

0 (0)

1,600 (488)

3,200 (975)

5,000 (1524)

6,600 (2012)

8,200 (2500)

Live near the surface, but can dive as deep as 9,000 feet (2.7 km)

LOCATION

All tropical and temperate oceans. Mature males have even been seen near polar ice.

Blackdevil
ANGLER FISH

Several thousand feet below the surface of the sea, where it's darker than the deepest cave, lurks a creature right out of a horror movie—the blackdevil angler fish.

PERFECTLY UGLY

The blackdevil angler fish's round body hangs motionless in the water, its huge mouth gaping wide and studded with needle-like teeth. A structure like a tiny fishing rod pokes from its head, luring prey by casting a sickly, greenish glow. Luckily this fish isn't monster size, it's actually no bigger than a tennis ball!

It may not be beautiful, but the angler fish is perfectly suited for its pitch-black home. Down in the depths of the ocean, food is in short supply and this creature must be ready to swallow whatever prey it can get. Its huge mouth and stomach can stretch enough to allow it to eat victims twice its own size!

HIDDEN HORRORS

Camouflage is important to the blackdevil angler fish. Its red skin looks soot black in deep water where there's no light. The only visible part is its little "fishing rod," a sort of skinny fin. At the end of the rod is a small pocket holding a colony of microbes, whose bodies glow with a greenish light. The microbes get a safe home in this little pocket and, in return, the angler fish gets a glowing lure—another example of symbiosis.

But there are other smaller deep-sea creatures that glow in the dark with a similar greenish light (which is known as bioluminescence). Hungry predators come close to the angler fish's lure, mistaking it for easy prey—and instead end up as its dinner!

4 LET'S GO DIVING!

- TO PREPARE FOR YOUR DIVE, HOLD THE ANGLER FISH 3-D ACTION CARD UP TO YOUR WEBCAM.
- TO LOWER THE SUBMERSIBLE, PRESS THE **RETURN** KEY ON YOUR KEYBOARD.
- TO SEARCH FOR THE ANGLER FISH, **ROTATE** THE ACTION CARD TO THE LEFT AND RIGHT.
- PRESS THE **LEFT** KEY ON YOUR KEYBOARD TO WATCH A VIDEO OF THE ANGLER FISH.
- PRESS THE **RIGHT** KEY, THEN THE **NUMBER** KEYS, TO DISCOVER OTHER DEEP-SEA MONSTERS.

Frankenstein's fish

Male angler fish are smaller than your little finger, and instead of finding food, they concentrate on finding a female. They pick up the tiniest trace of her scent in the water, and when they find her they bite her side and join with her skin. Pretty soon all that's left of the male is a little tail sticking out of the female's side.

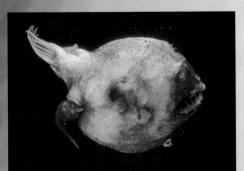

LEFT: The tiny male angler fish fuses with the body of the larger female.

Other deep-sea nightmares

Deep in the ocean's depths are many other creatures with faces not even their own moms could love! Try the triplewart sea devil, the female of which can weigh 22 pounds (10 kg), dwarfing the tiny 5-ounce (142 g) males. Or the umbrella mouth gulper, which lives more than a mile below the surface. All we know about many of these deep-sea monsters is what they look like. What they eat, how they breed, and how long they live remains a mystery.

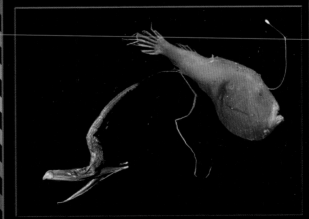

ABOVE: The umbrella mouth gulper (left) and the triplewart sea devil, another kind of angler fish (right).

SIZE

Up to 4 inches (10.2 cm)

DEPTH FT(M)

0 (0)

650 (198)

1,300 (396)

2,000 (610)

2,600 (792)

3,300 (1006)

Sometimes found in shallow water but prefers depths below 3,300 feet (1 km)

LOCATION

All the oceans of the world

OARFISH

For thousands of years, sailors have told tales of sea serpents with huge snake-like bodies and crested heads. But there is a real, live creature behind the legends—the oarfish.

SEA SERPENT

It may not be as powerful as Payanak, the sea serpent said to protect the country of Laos from enemies, but the oarfish is by far the longest bony fish in the ocean. Its body is like a giant, silvery ribbon and can grow to 50 feet (15.2 m) in length.

It's not only the oarfish's length and snakelike shape that links it to descriptions of sea serpents. It has a bright red fin stretching the length of its back, a tall crest on its head, and long red fins on either side. These striking features may have led to tales of maned sea monsters, and certainly earned the oarfish the name "king of the herrings."

ABOVE: Oarfish a known to ha motionless the wate

ABOVE: Could it be that the oarfish lies behind the many legends that exist about sea serpents?

 Into the future

Submarine technology is already giving exciting glimpses into the lives of oarfish and other deep-sea creatures. But there is so much more we can learn. Who knows what will be discovered next and who will discover it? Perhaps *you* will become the marine biologist or deep-sea explorer who will solve the mysteries of the oarfish—where it goes, what it does, and why it has a scarlet crown.